"Caitlin Johnson's *Delta* offers her readers a vision, at once both poetic and scientific, that serves to encourage and echo forward our calling to pay close attention to the world nearest us and the people with whom we surround ourselves. The collection offers a poetics of place, putting landscape, memory, and nature in conversation with ideas about war, history, chemistry (both scientific and romantic), and the canon. Her poems capture loss and joy, and invite readers to consider the ways our bodies, minds, and even souls are shaped by our space and our time. Her trilogy of poems featuring Joan of Arc, especially, highlights Johnson's ability to reflect truths, to create visions, and to embrace voices otherwise overlooked. I find her work engaging, exciting, and tense—in the best possible way. Each line, each image, each stanza is taut with meaning and significance, without relying on laborious or overwrought tones. Note the layered impact of her collection's title: *Delta*, with meanings related to science, mathematics, Classical culture, military culture, as well as Southern spaces. Cate's work consistently rewards multiple readings, varied considerations, and the careful, deliberate, and joyful approach of a reader looking for new ideas in conversation with old, elemental spaces."

-[Kristi Pope Key, Director of Academic Services, Louisiana School for Math, Science, and the Arts]

"Caitlin Johnson's *Delta* takes on a variety of subjects and themes—artistic, literary, scientific, and social—in a bold voice that is also darkly funny. She isn't like Plath, Sexton, or Parker; she is herself, but these poets come to mind. Interwoven throughout the book are lyrics inspired by the periodic table; snapshots of U.S. cities that convey place in just a few lines; ruminations on historical and literary figures—Joan of Arc, Macbeth—sympathetic but unsentimental portraits of soldiers; and (among my favorites) love and anti-love poems. "Letter to the Stepdaughter I Might Have Had" addresses a "you" who "hate[s] me. I can respect that," in the voiceof someone who may be too fiercely independent for the role of wife. In "Disappearances," an ex-lover "smelled of nothing— / nothing, & I wonder / if he existed at all. In *Delta*, Johnson distills her wide reading and life observations with candor and wit."

-[Deborah Diemont, author of *The Charmed House* and *Diverting Angels*]

Delta

$$\frac{y_2 - y_1}{x_2 - x_1} \left(= \frac{\Delta y}{\Delta x} \right)$$

Poems by Caitlin Johnson

Stubborn Mule Press
Devil's Elbow, MO

Copyright © Caitlin Johnson, 2021
First Edition: 1 3 5 7 9 10 8 6 4 2
ISBN:978-1-952411-82-3
LCCN:2021949942

Cover image: Caitlin Johnson
Author photos: Caitlin Johnson
All rights reserved. No part of this publication may be reproduced or transmitted in any form or by any means, electronic or mechanical, including photocopying, recording or by info retrieval system, without prior written permission from the author.

The following poems first appeared either in print or online:

"The Blue Hour": *Beans and Rice*. "Rn (86): *Dunes Review,* "The Gardener": *Dying Dahlia Review,* "Death of a Flower": *Foliate Oak Literary Magazine,* "Botanica" and "Taxonomy": *Foxglove Journal,* "Interview with Loki": *Wilderness House Literary Review,* "Letter to the Stepdaughter I Might Have Had": *The Furious Gazelle,* "La Pucelle" and "Saint Joan": *The Magnolia Review,* "Mary/Mary": *Melancholy Hyperbole,* "Doxology": *Mojave River Review,* "Earth's Edge," "In Another Life, a Farmer," "Pd (46)," "Sb (51)," and "Th (90)": *Now Then Magazine's Word Life* column, "5x5": *Pacifica Literary Review,* "Miss Havisham's Wedding Cake" and "The Seed of Fire": *Pembroke Magazine,* "The Swamp Fox": *Rejected Manuscripts,* "Things My Mother Never Taught Me": *Stoneboat Literary Journal,* "Chrismon": *TwentySomething Press,* "They Lack a Fundamental Understanding of Physics": *Visceral Uterus*

"Falsies" received an honorable mention in the non-rhyming poetry category in the 2016 Writer's Digest Annual Writing Competition.

"Cu (29)" won 20th place in the Writer's Digest 10th annual Poetry Awards.

"Dirty Old Man" and "Odyssea" each received honorable mentions in the non-rhyming poetry category in the 2019 Writer's Digest Annual Writing Competition.

The following poems first appeared in the chapbook *WAR/La Guerre:* "And Therefore We Will Not Be Accepting Your Application for the Position of Lady," "Cognizant," "Dermatology/Auguste Rodin," "Disappearances," "Falsies," "Far Enough West," "5x5," "Florence, SC," "The Gardener," "Interview with Loki," "Jeanne d'Arc," "La Pucelle," "Letter to the Stepdaughter I Might Have Had," "Praying to the Beast," "Razor," "Saint Joan," "S(h)elf Preservation," "The Swamp Fox," "Taxonomy," "Things My Mother Never Taught Me," and "The War in Reverse."

Table of Contents

Bennettsville II / 1

The Witches Speak / 2

The War in Reverse / 3

Po (84) / 4

Dermatology/Auguste Rodin / 5

Disappearances / 6

Earth's Edge / 8

Au (79) / 9

Cognizant / 10

Alms for the Poor / 11

Letter to the Stepdaughter I Might Have Had / 12

Fragment 3 / 13

Falsies / 14

Kitty Falls in Love / 15

They Lack a Fundamental
   Understanding of Physics / 16

Th (90) / 17

Miss Havisham's Wedding Cake / 18

Pd (46) / 19

Odyssea / 20

Sb (51) / 21

Jeanne d'Arc / 22

La Pucelle / 23

Saint Joan / 25

Algebra / 26

And Therefore We Will Not Be Accepting Your
   Application for the Position of Lady / 27

Rn (86) / 28

In the Aftermath / 29

Cu (29) / 30

The Hunting Wood / 31

Death of a Flower / 32

Fragment 1 / 33

GOD / 34

Florence, SC / 35

Chrismon / 36

Fe (26) / 37

The Swamp Fox / 38

The Scientist / 40

Taxonomy / 41

Far Enough West / 43

Razor / 44

S(h)elf Preservation / 45

The Gardener / 46

Ar (18) / 47

5x5 / 48

Praying to the Beast / 50

Answers to a Test I'm Failing / 51

In Another Life, a Farmer / 53

Co (27) / 54

The Prettiest Star / 55

Hoover Dam: Nevada Side / 56

Ra (88) / 57

Interview with Loki / 58

Ti (22) / 59

Natchitoches II / 60

Thou Shalt Be / 61

Orpheus / 62

Fragment 2 / 63

Conjuring / 64

The Seed of Fire / 65

Things My Mother Never Taught Me / 66

The Blue Hour / 67

Dirty Old Man / 68

Solid-state Reaction / 70

Domicile / 71

Mg (12) / 72

Botanica / 73

Doxology / 74

Eu (63) / 75

To Lisa, contemplator of cats.

Even though I've seen the end and I've had enough, / I can't make it stop. [Charlotte O.C.]

Bennettsville II

I need to know how many
                              years
you'll live inside
                my bones,
breaking them
because the bending
                        is not enough.

The Witches Speak

We whisper to him
                            Macbeth
because duty dictates it.

Hail, Macbeth.

Our gruesome news
rises from the cauldron
in undulating smoke.

Thou shalt be king.

The cracked mud caking his boots
is as useful to us as holy water.
We would have his severed head.

Hail, Macbeth.

Yes, hail.
He will bring us more blood
than all the black bats in our cave.

Thou shalt be king.

The king of death among warriors.
The evergreen fallen under its own weight.
The man undone.

Hail.

The War in Reverse

I always meet them
after they've come home—
uniforms relinquished, medals conferred,
scars gone or hidden at least.

& what do I know of war?
I see camouflaged men on the street,
failing to forge alliances with anyone
outside a platoon.
They don't speak to me; I don't question them.
I don't think much of them.

Then some trickle into my life,
like the water they craved
or the blood they lost
in the sandbox that was never
like the ones in their own backyards.

Scorpions and camel spiders, they tell me—
these are the worst things they saw.
3500-calorie MREs—the worst
things they swallowed.
Rocks heavier than cows—
the worst they carried.

Their nightmares buried,
wounds ignored, as if they were still
recruits afraid of drill sergeants,
who were the scariest guys on Earth.

Po (84)

> *Alexander Litvinenko died in 2006 after ingesting polonium-210. His murder was political.*

"Assassin's choice,"
the President tells you,
& this is what you decide:
> skip the anemia, the leukemia;
> use the instantaneous, the acute.

Irradiate the city
while you wait for your friend
> to sip his tea.
Geiger will not betray you.

Dermatology/Auguste Rodin

This isn't like
        a Rodin sculpture,
all bronze & solid & just—
I mean, he really knew how
to capture those fine lines.
Baudelaire & Balzac, their craggy skin
        so fucking real
        even in metal—
look, if I could have
        seen those things
showing through my own mask
from the start,
maybe fear wouldn't be
        pooling around my orbitals now.

Disappearances

I. *Brainwashed*

Check it:
you're not you,
& everything you know
is wrong.

II. *Suicide Risk*

These endless red fieds.

Maybe if I don't move,
I will cease to exist,
dissolve into burnt sienna
& alloy my dust with the dirt
before I run out of skin
to give away.

III. *Ex-Lover*

He smelled of nothing—
nothing, & I wonder
if he existed at all.

IV. Shipwrecked

Please
do
not
seek
me
(stop)
I
want
to
be
here
(stop)

Earth's Edge

The tide pulls the water
& the water pulls me
ceaselessly, toward the edge
of the world.

They say it's not flat—
science has proven so—
but I know it ends somewhere
& I alone in my skiff
am destined to fall
off the map
into some black saltwater abyss.

Au (79)

In me there is a hint of gold,
a dissolving Midas touch.
Everything I handle falls down:
a tree gutted by beetles,
a house in hurricane wind,
grass warped under the sun.

My kingdom, a dying ecosystem.

Cognizant

       (Tick-
I've been bumped out back
to await the news.
       tock.)

They pack mother into her shroud.

Hers is the lone silent face
in the midst of ululation.
The shrieking grows.
My father growls. My brother moans.
This, my home.

Alms for the Poor

There is nothing about me that sparkles:
a destitute girl
with dead irises, palest skin.
I collect what I can, these
alms for the poor.
They stymie me & weigh
down my soul-propelled bones,
delicate tendons stretched
too far to support the burden.
Little church mouse is better off
without your collection plate.

Letter to the Stepdaughter I Might Have Had

You hate me. I can respect that.
After what your momma did to your daddy—
the lies like frozen honey, too cloudy
to look through—you can't trust
a woman near him, like you have
an allergic reaction from proximity
alone, no need for a sting.

Darlin', I'm not squabbling with you
or trying to buzz through your brain,
humming like some kind of queen
bee, asserting my superiority
whenever you enter my hive.

Think of him as the flower, me as the winged
creature drawn to his nectar. I worship
the nourishment he gives. Together
we'll produce what your momma never could:
sugar so pure it melts.

Fragment 3

& them Oklahoma boys—
trust them as far as you can kick 'em,
but not as far as they can kick you.

Falsies

No one has eyelashes like that,
        except you.
We thought they were
        fake,
        pasted on,
        thick with mascara & permanent marker,
because boys aren't meant
to be that beautiful.

The closer we got, the less real they looked.
& when you disappeared,
        we expected to find
        a pile of tiny hairs
        left behind
        where you had sat.

Kitty Falls in Love

Faded freckles scattered over your arms,
& soft fingertips like suede:
under such an embrace, I become
your docile kitten.

They Lack a Fundamental Understanding of Physics

He speaks of the (im)possibility
of love: something almost like time
travel: i.e., theoretical: i.e.,
accessible to alien creatures
he can't (won't) understand.
She says, "I'm no scientist," which
means, "Let's find the fourth
dimension together," which means,
"I can prove you wrong & you'll
like it when I do."
He shakes his head, admits
telescopes scare him as much
as microscopes = observation frightens
him = the fear of change.
She sighs. Δ is how she lives
her life, lest she should turn
supernova & throw her own self
out of orbit, suck them both
into a black hole.

Th (90)

They call us hurricanes,
these girls with storms in our brains.
But we were born of thunder:
silver streaking into black.
& we never disappear—
just make our circuit
on high,
hoping for the days
when we're able to blaze.

Miss Havisham's Wedding Cake

She was eccentric even then,
before the heartbreak of the missing groom.
When she ordered up her cake,
my staff trembled: thirteen tiers,
a height none of us had reached.
The flavor she chose was plain white,
but the exterior—you never saw
such a mélange. Gilded doves
circled violet rosettes on a forest-green
backdrop, burgundy lattice edging each layer.
She insisted on these deep colors,
swore they symbolized something,
though she never said what.
It's possible she'd had a premonition
of the decay to come, but that day
in my bakery, she looked fiery
& indefatigable, her blue eyes bright,
her black hair glossy, her pink lips
still free from shrivel. People tell me
the cake remains on her table—
collapsing, a pastry Tower of Pisa.
Maggots nest in it now, & sometimes
in her hair, too: the jilted woman.

Pd (46)

I want to feel magical again—
not this hard silver shell
cold in the night.

Let me be pooling moonlight
until the shadows dissipate
from my witchcraft.

Odyssea

I've been out of my own life
for decades now:
Odyssea, they should call me,
the girl lost in a sea
roiling dark & stormy.

Impossible to recall the rolling dunes
along the shore; all I see
is ocean pooling around me,
crashing across me each rough night.

& so what if I never come home?
Who searches for me?
There are blond-haired children
poised as replacements,
ready to play out an existence I missed
by falling into the dim waters so young.

Sb (51)

I fumble for the kohl.
My eyes will be blacker
than my own unsteady
mind tonight.

No one must see me
without this heavy armor—
a smoldering look
the only defense
a woman has.

Jeanne d'Arc

We find her suspicious.
What girl knows these things?
What peasant knows these things?
What peasant cares?

We are men.
We are superior.
Yes, God is with us,
but no—we don't need her
telling us what He thinks.
We can make those judgments
for ourselves,

& we will,
& she will not.

La Pucelle

I. *She Hears a Voice*

like Moses before her,
& she doubts nothing:
this is her God.
The upending of her life,
the black spots on the road ahead—
these will never deter her.

The words fall easily into her brain.
The prophecies fall easily from her mouth.

II. *She Dreams of a King*

& she means to meet him,
replace that absent crown.
The glorious tension between her face
& her aim intrigues the men.
They lead her to the dauphin's door.

III. *She Begins to Fail*

A girl both decisive & divisive
comporting herself in ways unbecoming of a demoiselle
finds herself losing the unmatched potency
of her early visions.

IV. *She Is Condemned*

Fire makes us pure, the priests say,
but we see her defiled there,
her fortitude seared away
by this reverse baptism.
There is nothing fancy about it;
the church has abandoned its aesthetics
to teach us our place.

The world flutters away
in ashes.
Never an old woman.

Saint Joan

C'est magnifique,
these flames:

              the things I've been needing.

I am
the flame.

       Je suis la flamme.
       Je suis la femme.
       Non. Je suis la pucelle.

Rouen: the place to die,
the place to try.
La place pour l'histoire.

God, I adore you
for sending me here.
This—this is it.
What I wanted.
For you,
& for me.

Algebra

She is unsolvable,
        & that is that.

No more a question
to be answered,
        only a forgotten problem:
this way, that way,
solve for X—

but any way,
        it didn't matter.
She wasn't what
you thought she was,
& your equations could
        never
        never
        never
add her up.

And Therefore We Will Not Be Accepting Your Application for the Position of Lady

I.

Oh, no.
She won't do at all

She: recalcitrant.
We: ever so mannered.

II.

We are seeking good girls.
However, at this time,
we have strong doubts
about your ability to metamorphose
into a proper specimen
of femininity.

You see the problem, of course.

Rn (86)

I come from
>decay,
the pieces my never-siblings
left behind:
>salvaged from two
>& made Gemini.

Everyone calls me
>an old soul,
as if I've existed
billions of years,
but I die
>all the time,
a chain of breakdowns
like the ones
>before.

In the Aftermath

It was like
the slow recovery
after a nap:
the throb & shock,
the irrevocable feeling
of having been
misplaced.

Cu (29)

The copper came
when the rift was done,
the depths of that seismic hole
pushing up verdigris
& tawny bronze
like some new tree.
But I think it's been in me
from the start:
curling through my insides
where I could already sense
its soft edges, its sharp heart.

The Hunting Wood

- Julian, patron saint of hunters

I. *Summer*

Here I see the green
& the greenery:
ferns carpeting the forest floor,
a canopy overhead—
enveloped by bounty.

II. *Autumn*

Here I see the brown
& the bronzed:
leaves crumpling underfoot,
tree bark rough to the touch—
surrounded by decay.

III. *Winter*

Here I see the white
& the whiteout:
sky bleached thin,
bounding snow blanketing all—
encircled by Heaven.

IV. *Spring*

Here I see the blue
& the bluebird:
forget-me-nots forging a path,
the winged reaching for treetops—
invested by grace.

Death of a Flower

We should be free or we should die,
    but freedom is death

                             sometimes—
when the world opens up
like a flower, petals of possibility
splayed before you, each

                             opportunity
waiting to be
               plucked
               examined
               admired
& you're so long in choosing
that the flower withers
                         & dies,
brown at the edges.

None of us mean to kill it, & so
we force our own demise

                        to make up for it.

Fragment 1

In my face, the child
sees a prophet.
Never so much luck.

GOD

God is corroded,
a death's-head with gaping eyes.
I would rather Walt Whitman,
his Biblical strands of words & Mosaic beard.
Or give me a young dude
with a sprig of grain & a cowboy's gait.
Never soulless GOD, thunderous Zeus—
always the prism & the light.

Florence, SC

You are the chapter
& the verse,
      & I—
      I am the curse.

Chrismon

Scribbling Christograms—
the X both cross and Christ—
never did me much good.
What I need is a bit
of the god himself:
a dove or a rock,
a soft-scaled fish,
or the breeze blowing
so my hair floats
toward heaven, giving me
reason to look
at the light.

Fe (26)

I met a boy with
gray eyes
& I wondered
from whence
that steel
came.

The Swamp Fox

I.

South Carolina: late summer.
The fox waits.
Daisies in the field, ash on the wind.
Others will come.
The world tilts in a direction
no one expects but him.

II.

The fox: creature of wile,
emissary of rebellion.
He sets the fires.
He was built to destroy.
He cannot wait for time's entropy
to do the job.

III.

Daisies: dead now.
The horde awaits the fox's failure,
but he is become amphibian, alluvial.
What unnecessary days they waste,
hoping for him
to let his world fall down.

IV.

The others: nothing like him.
He smells the fear in their meat,
vile & turbid. Unfocused.
Instinct tells him to mangle.

V.

The world is his: cypress,
shallow waters, moss.
He will drown them, his lawlessness
transformed into righteousness.
The air grows heavy with adrenaline.

VI.

No one: a fox undone.
Limbs strewn, hunger unsated,
he fumbles now.
The verdant days have disappeared.

The Scientist

Life shrinks around you
until all you can see
is the bright slide under the microscope.

& what is there:
the microorganisms that control you,
the bloodless bustling of a tiny world.

Zoom in.
More.
   More.
        More.

The slide cracks.
All is lost.

Taxonomy

Domain: *Eukaryota*

It's not just the nucleus:
it's the membrane-envelope
keeping us from oozing out;
it's the matriarchal mitochondria
tracing us back before even Eve.

Kingdom: *Animalia*

Sometimes we forget
that we are animals, too—
we love to expunge
the evidence.

Phylum: *Chordata*

Musculature is not enough.
We need to grow a fucking backbone,
prove ourselves capable of contortions.

Class: *Mammalia*

We reject the reptilian brain.
We reject the scaled skin.
We reject the gills.

We demand the milk.

Order: *Primates*

Little fingers, little tails.
Eyes that seem to know.
& we hide in the trees.

Family: *Hominidae*

& what is so great
about the Great Apes?
The bonobos, the gorillas, the chimpanzees—sure.
But then comes the fourth.

Genus: *Homo*

Struggling to become upright/upstanding/upheavers.
Striding into the scrum.
Leaving antiquity, entering the man-made universe.

Species: *H. sapiens*

It's not enough to conquer.
We must humiliate, as well:
subjugate, colonize, destroy.
The natural world?
No. The human one.

Far Enough West

If you move   far enough west,
                          far enough south,
you will outrun him.
But one day, you'll have   no more land,
                                   no more road,
& you'll be stuck on a shoreline
somewhere unfamiliar,   no docks,
                          no boats.
There, he catches up.
There, you learn about futility.

Razor

He scrapes at me:
sharp metal man,
the edge of his body a thin
blade. He cuts into my hip,
draws color to the surface.
Droplets bubble up: lipstick/
crimson/burgundy red, rolling
down my pale legs
toward the beacon of him,
traveling through an invisible
tube from my body
to his—accident or transfusion?—
staining him pink, an angry blotch.

S(h)elf Preservation

You taste
like Fighting Cock straight from the bottle:
the burn,
        the enchantment,
                the barrage.
A specious unguent.
You should be formaldehyde instead,
                    pickle me
in a jar for your shelf.

The Gardener

If I could plunge my hands
into the soil here in my Northern backyard
& reach all the way to your Southern abode,
believe me, darlin', I would,
just to brush the tips of your fingers,
exchange some of my lake sand
for some of your ocean sand, the chance
to smell your salt on the air again.

Ar (18)

We are noble,
or we try to be:
dignified, floating above all,
but straining against our shells.

& so we go on like this,
hovering near each other:
an abundance of potential
terrified to react.

5x5

I. *Pfc/Army*

He was
an alcoholic, even at that
young age. Spoiled, aimless,
eyes out of focus
no matter where his gaze settled.

II. *PO2/Navy*

Honorably discharged
but learned nothing about
discipline. Knew only
about sailors' knots
& escaping out to sea.

III. *A1C/Air Force*

Bored, always moving
his hands to keep his mind
from wandering into
dark places where he might
have to face the world's truth.

IV. *Sgt/Army*

This secretive, mysterious
paratrooper was not afraid

to jump, but I wonder
if he could ever
pull the cord.

V. *SSgt/Army*

His scope on the distance,
scouting because he can't stop.
Every attempt I make
to draw him back into me
works momentarily, then fails.

Praying to the Beast

"Save me," I say,
but he says, "No."

Maybe if I were Catholic,
full of Hail Marys
& smelling of Amazing Grace—

but the only hallelujahs I know
are the broken ones,
& none of it matters at all.
My (false) beliefs
weren't ever going to save my soul.

Answers to a Test I'm Failing

1) Sometimes I dream about you.

2) Oh, that wasn't the question?
   I'm sorry;
   I get distracted sometimes.

3) By what?
   L'amour, of course.

> *sigh*

4) Yes, I realize that's a strong word.

5) How empty are you
   if you never felt it?

6) Sorry.
   You're the one asking the questions.

> *sigh*

7) Did I ever tell you
   how the disquiet in my brain
   melted away?

8) No, I wasn't Prozac-happy, sex-happy.
   I was actually happy.

9) So this, you see,
   is what you wrested from me.

10) Of course I don't blame you.
    Entirely.

    laugh

11) You incinerated me.
    I know you know that.

12) All right. Let's call it my fault.
    I'm the one who started it, after all.

In Another Life, a Farmer

It was the fecundity,
what brought you this way.
Your nature pushed you
toward the wild, the unmanicured,
the ample fields, the spread-out land:
the reproductive possibilities,
the thrill of taming.

Co (27)

Every time I try to describe
your eyes, I get it wrong.

Glacial? No.
The Louisiana sky on a bright day?
That's closer to it.

They're like marbles
that were meant to be clear,
but someone's hand slipped
& cobalt dust melted into the glass:
that hint of color,
an accidental tinge,
& they are
liquid-lovely.

The Prettiest Star

- for Christopher Wells

The cigarette death wasn't working—
those tiny red buds don't burn hot enough,
& cancer takes too long.

You became supernova instead,
bursting black, collapsing at the center.
Dying stars can't contain themselves.

Sometimes I am angry
that you left such a space in the sky,
more black hole than celestial sparkle.

But I never ask why.
I know how oblivion looks
to the lonely space traveler.

Hoover Dam: Nevada Side

This is the wall that will kill me. Concrete one thousand feet down to gushing waters. The violence of drowning after breaking.

Ra (88)

- Maria Skłodowska/Madame Curie 1867-1934

French now,
but always of Polonia—
no matter what the Russians,
               the Germans,
               the Hungarians say.

But I won't go home again.
The chemicals flow in me,
& I glow, though I pale.
               I am become
               the isotope itself.

Interview with Loki

It's like,
>shit, man,
>y'all are taking this
>too seriously, you know?

& sometimes they're just
asking too much—
as if letting my soul die
will somehow help the world.

I'm not the killer here.
I'm only the one
trying to tear the bitches down,
but then,
>the uncertainty principle
>always did freak them out.

Look at me. Do I seem
unhinged to you?
No.
  I'm unfettered.

Ti (22)

They label me bloodless.
I cannot change that which I am.

Prophecy is the truth
cast into the wild,
cold white.

& I: unyielding augur.

Natchitoches II

I wished for the slow skiving off, the precision of a scientist
    who would cauterize me—
        flesh charred & purified at once, ready to be cut again.
But if you slice me open now, you'll see what I meant
        when I said I can't be near knives anymore.

Thou Shalt Be

- Macbeth, 1.3

The good & bad of my life,
the hope & despair.
The learned lover & faulty guide.
The fire
        & also the ash.

Seek me one thousand times more
as my castle falls.
I will be gone,
but you are Invictus,
& thou shalt be king hereafter.

Orpheus

How am I meant to write about him
when I can't even see his face?
He won't look at me any more than he'll eye Eurydice,
preferring instead to play his music-games.

How can I describe anything other than
the tilt of the back of his head as it recedes
toward the light, leaving the rest of us behind?

How should I convey his jauntiness, his sheer cheek
as he bounces away from Hades,
thinking he's made a fine deal?
What of the other souls who won't be rescued?

No, Orpheus.
I will not share you with the world
until you liberate me, too.

Fragment 2

I know it's there—
just　　　　　beyond.

& when it comes,
you better
　　　　　　run
　　　　　　　　boy
　　　　　　　　　　run.

Conjuring

> *By the pricking of my thumbs, /*
> *something wicked this way comes.*
>   - Macbeth, 4.1

Tiptoeing around the flames
at first:
plaintive & earnest as the early leaves
scattered across the undergrowth.

I conjure you, fire.
I request magic.

No, I demand magic:
hands fluttering above my head,
undulating hair mimicking fire itself.

And a yawp,
a cat-hiss,
a screeching from inside me
comes to make my point:
I will have my power.

The Seed of Fire

From a line by Thomas Heffernan

Consider the eaten half of an apple,
the negative space   it leaves behind.
Now imagine it as a void   inside me,
growing larger   each time you bite.

But you refuse the tiny black kernels,
thinking them trash.

                A waste.

This ravaged landscape is my garden,
& you have left me

                these seeds of fire.

Watch them blossom here:
poison apples, & I,

                poised for revenge.

Things My Mother Never Taught Me

It wasn't her fault, I don't think.
But her own mother failed,
& so she faltered, unsure pilot
on the turbulent waters of my youth.

The missing things
haunt me now: fog on the surface,
obscuring my view so my journey
upstream is fraught;
I hit rocks, run my rudder
onto banks, lose items overboard.

Some don't matter much—
burdens cast off so I don't sink.
But how do I know when
to throw a life preserver down
& save a drowning man?
He might pull me in.

& if I stray into straits
cut through with sandbars,
should I turn back to navigate
a different path? If the river
forks, do I drop anchor
to make my decision slowly,
or will I take on water that way?

She never says. I'll never know.

The Blue Hour

Lazy Saturday.
Light steals into the room
through the space between
the top of the blinds
& the top of the window.
Everything is azure.

It's called the blue hour,
I think, but only because
my walls are ocean.
If they were chartreuse,
it would be the green
hour; crimson, the red.

So I lie
here on my black bedspread,
contemplating the way dust
scatters, transforming my cyan scene
into something more grayscale.

Dirty Old Man

Let me tell you about sex,
he says,
         & I blush,
because he means
what my friends do not
with their penis jokes & guffaws
when a girl giggles at their words.

No, he means making love.
He means seduction—
the old way, as if
I might be waiting around the corner
to slip off my seamed stockings
one
     agonizing
               inch
at a time.

& when I quaver, he laughs
his throaty chuckle.
You remind me of the old-country girls
who know how to be coy,
girls who never fidget at the prospect
of undressing,
              of being naked in this world.

He makes me feel illicit,
& I want to be illicit:

    throbbing center of someone's
          after-dark life,
    the pleasure at the end of the show.

    I want to be in that indecent world,
    immaculate in my blonde dishabille,
    my hair flowing over his chest
                          like smut.

Solid-state Reaction

First: ensure the materials
can be mixed. Eliminate volatility.
Then: see how they fall together
in their self-made crucible.
Next: watch them melt into one
as heat is applied.
Finally: marvel at the crystals
springing up around them.

This is what we call chemistry.

Domicile

"This is where I live now,"
I whispered, & I didn't mean
in that blue room, that walnut-wood bed.

I meant in the tiny cleft of your chin,
the skin you wear, the very veins
supplying your life,
making myself domestic to your body.

Mg (12)

Across the street, generators—
but here, only candles glow.
I will find you through the dim,
illuminate you resplendent:
a beacon in this austerity.
Nothing can extinguish me now.

Botanica

& have we grown together—
the vine & the tree,
our own ecosystem evolving around us?
Your oxygen, my chlorophyll,
green & hushed in the sunset:
feeding the world, forming ourselves.
My garden. Your garden.

Doxology

Let this be my doxology, then:
    I see your face
           in my dreams
        sometimes, unaware
          it belongs to you.
    But I feel your touch
          in the morning:
          my first conscious inhalation
          came from you.
    & I remember the sensation
          in my chest then,
        the way my lungs swell
        even at rest,
the joy of you.

Eu (63)

You are   a continent
         to me,
full of history
              I may never learn,
spun by time
into a thin silver line
         stretching from decade

                              to decade,
& ductile still.

Caitlin Johnson is the author of three chapbooks and one previous full-length collection of poetry. She holds an MFA from Lesley University and lives in Michigan.